Project Tiger

Susan Ring

Weigl Publishers Inc.

Editor
Diana Marshall

Design and Layout
Warren Clark
Bryan Pezzi

Copy Editor
Jennifer Nault

Photo Researcher
Tina Schwartzenberger

Published by Weigl Publishers Inc.
123 South Broad Street, Box 227
Mankato, MN 56002 USA
Web site: www.weigl.com

Library of Congress Cataloging-in-Publication Data

Ring, Susan.
  Project Tigernew / Susan Ring.
     p. cm. -- (Zoo life)
Summary: Showcases the development and growth of a baby tiger at a zoo, discussing the zookeeper's role in its life and the natural habitat, foods, and life cycle of the animal.
  ISBN 1-59036-015-X (lib. bdg. : alk. paper)
  1. Tigers--Infancy--Juvenile literature. 2. Zoo animals--Indiana--Indianapolis--Juvenile literature. [1. Tigers. 2. Animals--Infancy. 3. Zoo animals.] I. Title. II. Zoo babies (Mankato, Minn.)
  QL737.C23 R56 2002
  599.756'139--dc21

2002006395

Printed in the United States of America
1 2 3 4 5 6 7 8 9 0   06 05 04 03 02

Photograph Credits
Every reasonable effort has been made to trace ownership and to obtain permission to reprint copyright material. The publishers would be pleased to have any errors or omissions brought to their attention so that they may be corrected in subsequent printings.

Cover: baby Amur tiger (Photo Courtesy of the Indianapolis Zoo); **Photos Courtesy of the Indianapolis Zoo:** title page, pages 3, 4, 5, 6, 7, 8, 9, 10, 11, 12, 13, 14, 15, 19 right, 21; **D. Robert & Lorri Franz:** pages 18, 22 top, 23; © **Joel Sartore/CORBIS/MAGMA:** page 17 right; **David Welling:** pages 16, 17 far left, 17 left, 17 middle, 17 far right, 19 left, 20, 22 bottom.

The Species Survival Plan® is a registered conservation program of the American Zoo & Aquarium Association.

Contents

Babies are Born

One night in late July, a rare **Amur tiger** gave birth to three baby tigers. A **tigress** at the Indianapolis Zoo became the proud mother of one male and two female cubs. The baby tigers were very small. It was hard for the **zookeepers** to believe that the cubs would weigh 100 pounds in only a few months.

Zoo Issues

Should newborn baby animals be put on public display?

The tiny, helpless baby tiger looked like a kitten when she was born.

Like all tigers, the cubs were born with their eyes and ears closed. Within 1 hour, the cubs were drinking their mother's milk. A few hours later, zoo **veterinarians** checked the baby tigers to make sure they were healthy. The cubs were **vaccinated** to prevent them from becoming sick.

The zoo did not show the mother and her babies to visitors right away. It waited almost 8 weeks until the cubs were bigger and stronger.

BRAIN BOOSTERS

- Baby tigers are called cubs.

- Mother tigers usually have two or three cubs at one time. The mother tiger cares for them by herself.

- In the wild, tiger cubs are usually born between March and July.

- At birth, tiger cubs weigh between 2 and 3 pounds. Newborn tigers are 12 to 16 inches in length.

- A mother tiger licks her newborn cubs clean with her rough tongue.

For the first 8 weeks, a video camera called "tiger cam" allowed zoo visitors to view the tiger family without disturbing them.

Meet the Babies

Zookeepers named the cubs. Since Amur tigers are found in Russia, they chose Russian names. One female was named Pahstrel, which means "imp." The zookeepers chose this name because she was playful and curious. Pahstrel's sister was named Shastyah, which means "happiness." The male cub was named Vachno, which means "important."

Should baby zoo animals share enclosures with their mother? Why?

All three cubs were very active and playful.

- Amur tigers are also called Siberian tigers. They live in the cold, snowy woodlands of Russia and parts of Asia.

- Amur tigers are the largest of all the tigers.

- Amur cubs drink their mother's milk for 6 to 8 weeks. Little by little, they learn to eat the solid food she brings back from her hunting trips.

- Tiger cubs grow quickly. Sometimes, they will gain almost 1 pound each day.

- It takes tiger cubs between 6 and 14 days to open their eyes. Their ears open after about 10 days.

At birth, Pahstrel, Shastyah, and Vachno each weighed a little more than 2 pounds. They grew very quickly. Like tigers in the wild, the cubs could not walk right away. They crawled around the **enclosure** for 3 weeks until their legs were strong enough to support their bodies. After 6 weeks, they started to eat solid food. The tigress licked her cubs clean and groomed them often. The baby tigers spent 20 hours of each day sleeping.

It took Pahstrel and her siblings 2 weeks to grow their baby teeth. These are called milk teeth.

Teaching Tigers

For the first months, veterinarians checked the cubs every few weeks. As they became older, the cubs received medical care only when needed. At the Indianapolis Zoo, a mother tiger raises her cubs on her own if she is able. Zookeepers knew that the tigress was capable and loving. So, they allowed her to care for her babies on her own. Zookeepers were never in the enclosure with the mother and cubs.

The tigress taught her cubs to clean themselves and play. The cubs watched their mother closely. They were learning to **stalk** and pounce. They were learning hunting skills.

Zoo Issues

Why is it important for zoo food to be similar to animals' food in the wild?

In the zoo, the cubs did not have to hunt for food. This left more time for the cubs to play with each other.

Brain Boosters

- In the wild, tiger cubs learn how to hunt at 5 to 6 months of age. Their mother shows the cubs what **prey** to eat and how it can be caught.

- Amur tigers may live with their mother for 4 years before they are ready to leave.

- When teaching her cubs to hunt, a mother tiger will show them how to walk quietly. It is important that tigers are quiet when they hunt so they can surprise their prey.

Zookeepers bring the cubs their food. Still, the Indianapolis Zoo provides toys, such as meaty bones, to keep their hunting **instincts** alive. Different smells within the enclosure keep the tigers alert and active. The cubs learned to climb rocks, jump across branches, and swim. They also **adapted** to people. The cubs moved into and out of the enclosure every morning and evening to let the zookeepers enter. They learned that if they want dinner, they must go inside the building to get it.

Meet the Parents

The cubs' mother is named Lena. She was found in Russia in 1992, when she was a tiny tiger cub. Lena's mother was killed by **poachers**, leaving four cubs motherless. Lena was brought to the United States as part of the Tiger Species Survival Plan (SSP). She was sent to the Indianapolis Zoo in 1993.

Zoo Issues

Should breeding in zoos be controlled and monitored?

■ Lena's close ties to the wild made her an important addition to the Amur tiger breeding program.

- Female tigers are ready to mate at about 3 years of age. Male tigers are ready when they are 4 or 5 years old.

- A mother tiger gently carries her cubs in her mouth, one by one. Holding on to the loose skin on their neck and part of their head, the mother moves her cubs from den to den. The cubs know to go limp. They do not struggle or make a sound.

- Tigers are solitary animals. This means they live and hunt alone. They leave **scents** and claw trees to mark their **territory**.

- Tigers come together to mate between November and April.

The cubs' father, Dshingis, came to the Indianapolis Zoo in 1996. Dshingis and Lena were introduced in hopes that they would mate. They were part of a special **breeding program** to save the Amur tigers.

In the wild, when a tigress is ready to have her babies, she finds a well-hidden **den**. This den is far from the male, so that the cubs can be born in safety. When Lena was ready to give birth, she was moved to a private den, away from the other tigers and zoo visitors.

Dshingis was born in a zoo in Germany.

Furry Friends

Since they are solitary animals, it is never certain how two tigers will react to each other. For this reason, Lena and Dshingis were carefully introduced from opposite sides of a secure enclosure. Slowly, they adjusted to each other's smells and sounds. When they were put in the same enclosure, they naturally came together to breed. Lena and Dshingis still get along very well.

Zoo Issues

Think of some reasons why zoo animals may need to be separated.

■ While the cubs were young, Lena raised them on her own. Their father was kept in a separate enclosure.

Now a handsome adult tiger, Kolyma is important to the zoo's tiger breeding program.

To prevent fights over territory or injury to the cubs, Dshingis lived in a separate enclosure. The tigers at the zoo are grouped by their age and how well they get along with others.

Pahstrel and her siblings were not the first cubs born to Lena and Dshingis. Two male cubs were born in 1998. They were named Kolyma and Kavacha, after regions in Russia. Kavacha was sent to another zoo for breeding. The other cubs will stay at the Indianapolis Zoo until the SSP committee decides where each cub should go for breeding.

BRAIN BOOSTERS

- The Indianapolis Zoo's breeding program is part of the American Zoo & Aquarium Association's Species Survival Plan. This program is designed to save **endangered** species, such as the Amur tiger, from **extinction**.

- In 1994, there were only 200 Amur tigers in the wild. Since then, **conservation** groups have worked to protect these animals. Today, about 400 Amur tigers live in the wild.

The Zoo Crew

The Amur tigers live in an 8,130-square-foot open enclosure that copies their natural **habitat**. The tigers can swim in a large, deep pool. A waterfall flows into a shallow nursery pool. Natural plant life helps the growing cubs feel like they are in the wild. There is an exercise yard out of public view that helps Pahstrel, Shastyah, and Vachno stay fit.

Rocks and trees fill the tiger enclosure. These features allow the cubs to climb and play.

Even though they are not handled by zookeepers, the cubs know them by scent and by sight.

Zookeepers feed and care for the tigers daily. The tiger cubs are very aware of the zookeepers. They know that zookeepers bring their food. Sometimes, the veterinarian gives the cubs medical care and cleans their teeth. Forest keepers and repair crews maintain the enclosure's plants, waterfalls, pools, and rocks.

HOW CAN I BECOME A VETERINARIAN?

A veterinarian's education depends on the area of animal care chosen. Students should study science and math. A college degree and love for animals are required. Animal care experience can be gained through volunteer work.

ZOO RULES

The Indianapolis Zoo's Amur tiger enclosure was designed to be a zoo without cages. Instead of glass walls, water, rocks, and wire separate people from the tigers. As long as visitors follow the zoo's rules, the tigers do not pay much attention to visitors. Zoos have rules that help keep animals and visitors safe and healthy.

Indianapolis Zoo's Rules:

1. Do not bring outside food into the zoo.
2. Do not feed the animals.
3. Stay on the pathways and off rocks, fences, and railings.
4. Do not damage or pick the plants on zoo grounds.
5. Pets are not allowed on the zoo grounds.

Animal Gear

Tigers are powerful and fast. Their orange fur and black stripes help them hide when they hunt for food. From their ears to their toes, tigers are built to be strong hunters.

Zoo Issues

Why should zoo enclosures be similar to an animal's natural habitat?

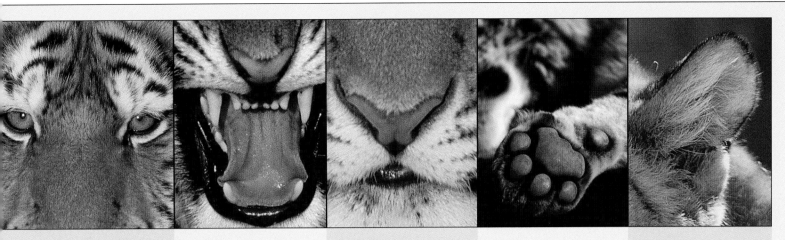

Eyes

Tigers have keen eyesight. In the dark, they can see six times better than humans. Tigers hunt at night or in dim light. This lets them surprise their prey. Like other **predators,** a tiger's eyes face forward. This helps them judge how far away their prey is.

Teeth

Tigers are carnivores. This means that they eat meat. Their **canine teeth** are long, sharp, and pointed. They help a tiger grip and tear the meat off bones. A tiger's jaw is so strong that it can crush a bone with one bite.

Nose

Tigers use their sense of smell to communicate. The scent they leave on trees and bushes lets other tigers know they are looking for a mate. A scent can also mark a tiger's territory. In the wild, tigers use their sense of smell to find food sources.

Paws

Tiger paws are covered in fur. On the bottom, their paws have padding. The fur and padding help tigers walk quietly as they hunt. Their 3- to 4-inch claws stay hidden when not in use. A hunting tiger will extend its claws to grip or tear its prey.

Ears

The tiger's excellent hearing is important to its survival. Tigers move their ears back and forth to identify and locate sounds. Tigers roar, purr, and growl. A tiger's roar can be heard from more than 1 mile away. Tiger cubs communicate with their mother by mewing.

In the Wild

Tigers spend most of their time hunting for food, such as wild pigs and deer. When little food is available, a tiger's territory will become larger. When tigers hunt prey, they do not run and chase it down the way some cats do. Instead, tigers slowly creep closer and closer. Then, they will suddenly pounce on the animal.

Sometimes, tigers must travel many miles to find enough to eat.

When female cubs grow up and leave their mother, they stay close to her territory. Male cubs will travel further away. They create new territories for themselves. An Amur tiger's territory can be as large as 300 to 390 square miles. All tigers must live close to water. They must also live near thick forests or grasslands where they can hunt.

BRAIN BOOSTERS

BRAIN BOOSTERS

- Tigers can eat more than 40 pounds of food in one meal.

- Amur tigers have very thick fur that keeps them warm in cold, snowy climates.

In the wild, a mother Amur tiger and her cubs will stay together for about 4 years or until more cubs are born.

- When a mother tiger returns from a hunt, she and her cubs greet each other with cuddles and licks.

Tigers Today

There are very few tigers left in the world. Less than 100 years ago, there were about 100,000 tigers in the wild. Now, there are fewer than 8,000 wild tigers. Humans hunted and killed tigers for many reasons. Some hunted for sport. Others used tiger bones in medicines. Some farmers had to protect their farm animals from hungry tigers. These tigers lost much of their territory to humans.

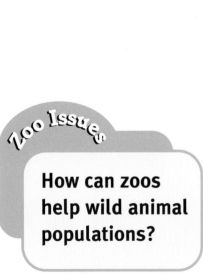

Zoo Issues

How can zoos help wild animal populations?

Of all the tigers living in the wild, only a few hundred are Amur tigers.

- Three types of tigers are extinct. These are the Caspian tiger, the Bali tiger, and the Javan tiger.

- The facts and features of each tiger are entered into a computer system. From this information, the SSP committee for tigers chooses which animals are put together to mate.

- In the wild, tigers live about 15 years. In zoos, tigers can often live to be 20 to 25 years old. This is because tigers in zoos have regular food and medical care.

- Hunting, habitat loss, and less prey are the main reasons for the decline in tiger populations. Humans are responsible for these three threats.

■ The hope is that cubs born in zoos will become parents in the tiger breeding programs.

The planet is close to losing tigers forever. Worldwide, conservation groups are working to save the Amur tigers. Information programs educate the people who live near wild tiger populations. The SSP is working to make sure that Amur tiger populations stay strong in zoos. It is also helping wild Amur tiger populations grow.

Tiger Issues

Benefits of Zoo Life

- No danger from predators, poaching, competition, or habitat loss
- Regular food, play time, and medical care
- Can help educate the public about tigers
- Is easier to research tigers in zoos
- Breeding programs maintain a stable zoo population
- Can live a longer life

Benefits of Life in the Wild

- More natural space in which to hunt and live
- Maintain diverse Amur tiger populations
- Daily mental and physical challenges, such as hunting
- Part of the natural web of life consisting of plants, predators, and prey
- Live complex lives
- Maintain independence

Folk Tale

The Hunter and the Tiger

Tiger folk tales can be found in the stories and songs of the people who share habitats with these big wild cats. One Siberian folk tale describes a boy who is not afraid of anything. One day, the boy traps a tiger. He lets it go free because he feels sorry for the tiger. The tiger changes into a boy and rewards his friend's kindness. The story is a reminder of the importance of treating the world's tigers with respect.

Source: Ginsburg, Mirra. *The Master of the Winds and Other Tales from Siberia.*
New York: Crown Publishers, 1970.

More Information

The Internet can lead you to some exciting information on tigers. Try searching on your own, or visit the following Web sites:

American Zoo and Aquarium Association (AZA)
www.aza.org

Indianapolis Zoo www.indyzoo.com

Kids for Tigers www.kidsfortigers.com

The Tiger Information Center www.5tigers.org

CONSERVATION GROUPS
There are many organizations involved in tiger research and conservation. You can get information on tigers by writing to the following addresses:

INTERNATIONAL
World Wildlife Fund
International
Avenue du Mont-Blanc
CH-1196, Gland
Switzerland

UNITED STATES
Hornocker Wildlife Institute
2023 Stadium Drive
Suite 1A
Bozeman, MT
59715

Words to Know

adapted: adjusted to new conditions

Amur tiger: one type of tiger that lives in the Amur River region of Russia, China, and North Korea

breeding program: producing babies by mating selected animals

canine teeth: long, pointed teeth, toward the front of the mouth

conservation: the care and monitoring of animals and animal populations for their continued existence

den: shelter of a wild animal

enclosure: closed-in area that is designed to copy an animal's home in the wild

endangered: animals whose numbers are so low that they are at risk of disappearing from the wild

extinction: complete disappearance

habitat: place in the wild where an animal naturally lives

instincts: things an animal knows naturally, without being taught

poachers: people who hunt and kill animals illegally

predators: animals that hunt and kill other animals for food

prey: animals that are hunted and killed for food

scents: smells an animal leaves behind

stalk: to slowly and quietly move toward something, such as prey

territory: area that an animal will defend as its own

tigress: female tiger

vaccinated: given medicines to prevent diseases

veterinarians: animal doctors

zookeepers: people at a zoo who feed and take care of the animals

Index